ADVENTURES OF

"Wild Bill"

DONOVAN

By

JOHN LAWRENCE DONOVAN

Copyright @ 2007 by John L. Donovan
Cover design by John L. Donovan
Book design by John L. Donovan
Publisher: John L. Donovan
All Rights Reserved

No part of this book may be reproduced in any form or by any electronic or mechanical means including information storage and retrieval systems, without the permission from the author.
The only exception is by a reviewer, who may quote short excerpts in a review.

John L. Donovan
Visit my Web Site at:
https://www.lulu.com/content/806156

ISBN: 978-0-6151-6716-9
Second Edition

Title: The Adventures of "Wild Bill" Donovan
Take a look at The Adventures of "Wild Bill" Donovan at:
https://www.lulu.com/content/806156

Chapter 1 The Early Years & World War One

Let us start at the beginning of William Pete's life. He was born to parents William S. Pete and Mary (Flora) LaFond on August 16, 1900 in the town of Ludlow, Massachusetts. His parents were married on July 26, 1899 in upstate Mooers, New York. The marriage appears in the Clinton County Marriage book of New York State.

The 1900 United States Census taken in April of 1900 lists the family residing on Elm Street, Ludlow, Massachusetts. Living at that address were the newlyweds, William S. Pete, age 19, and Flora LaFond, age 15. They are living with William S. Pete's brother Joseph and his wife Gertrude, and Flora's widowed mother Alice LaFond (Duval). To clear up the surname of LaFond---it is also used as Bottom. The English translation of LaFond is Bottom and will be used interchangeably. From the United States Census there is no listing of any occupation for William Pete, Jr.; therefore it is assumed that he was unemployed at that period of time. We later find that William and his family move back to Mooers, New York, where two daughters are born, Lillian in 1903 and Maude in 1905. Later in life Lillian plays an interesting and a big portion in William Pete, Jr's life.

In the 1910 United States Census we find William and his wife Flora living on a farm in Mooers, New York, with their children William, Jr., Lillian and Maude. William Sr. owns the farm and it is listed as farm # 46 of the supplemental farm schedule. Both William Sr., and Flora are able to speak and read English. Apparently William, Jr. got restless working on the farm and enlisted in the United States Army at Hartford, Connecticut on July 29, 1916, about three weeks before his sixteenth birthday. He lied to get into the Army and claimed he was born in 1897. While in the Army he was assigned to the 318th Engineers Train, and remained in the military until his discharge under honorable terms on October 14, 1919. He served in France during World War 1. His unit left the United States on May 8, 1918 and arrived in France on May 18, 1918. For his service, William now using the surname of Peterson, Jr. was awarded the WW1 Victory Button, and WW1 Victory Medal (Bronze).

Years later, in the 1930's he would receive a one-time pension for his brave service during World War 1. As mentioned above he changed his surname from Pete to Peterson. Many individuals who came to America from either Europe or from Nova Scotia, which is the place where the Pitre's came from changed their surnames to become more Americanized.

By the way, the ancestors of the Pete's were the Pitre's, who were Acadians who were exiled from France in the 1600's and some later settled in Nova Scotia, and then to Canada, to New England and some to Louisiana, they were called the Cajuns. The reason for the deportation of the Acadians was because the French did not like their fundamental Christian beliefs. If one wishes to pursue the history of the Pitre's and the Acadians, there are many books on the subject on the Acadians. One article written by Richard E. Chenard, titled "Acadia and the Acadians" appeared in the issues of the Morning Sentinel & Kennebec Daily Journal of Maine, on January 13, January 28 and February 11, 1995, and the article does a good job of the Acadian history.

When William, Jr., was discharged at Camp Grant in Illinois, his grade was Private First Class. William was given a bonus for his service during World War 1, which amounted to $60.00.

Other compensation was for clothing allowance and travel pay. The total muster out pay was $128.09, which was paid on December 23, 1921, just in time for Christmas of that year.

One item of interest is that a book was written on William's unit, the 318th Engineers, titled "The Life of Co. D, 318th Engineers" and was written by Charles M. Osborn. The book goes through the entire life of the 318th Engineers while serving in the United States and in France during World War 1, fighting in France, and the return of the unit to the United States to Camp Grant in Illinois and ends on the mustering of the troops beginning on June 18, 1919. The book titled "The Life of Co. D, 318th Engineers is available at the United States Army Heritage and Education Center, U.S. Army Military History Institute, 22 Ashborn Drive, Carlisle, PA 17013-5008. Since the book is old and that there is only one copy it cannot circulate out of the library; however, one can obtain a photocopy of it for a small fee.

We are going to embark on William's time spent in the United States Army while in the 318th Engineers Train from his training, and arrival in France in 1918, and the war against the Germans. William will encounter many hardships in the World War 1 Theater as well as did his Engineer group. This will take one from the landing in France to the construction of many bridges and warehouses as well as the many hikes the Engineers took into the war's front. It will show the hardships the members of the 318th Engineers would endure while fighting in the sector they were assigned to. They also dug trenches, galleries, and barbwire entanglements. The unit would be in actual combat and experience what war is really like. Then their return from the front and to the armistice that would occur on November 11th, 1918, and the return of the Engineer's unit to the United States and their muster out of the United States Army in June or later in 1919. This account was given in the book that is condensed below:

Excerpts from "The History of Company "D", 318th Engineers" Let us follow William Peterson's tracks as well as the other 249 troops of the 318th Engineers: Company D was formed at the Vancouver Barracks, Washington State as an organized unit on January 10th 1918. The Engineers were to be at full strength on about January 15th, with 250 men. The location of the Vancouver Barracks was a few hundred yards from the Columbia River, which separated Vancouver from the busy city of Portland, Oregon. The comforts, climate and people made for a great place for training of the Engineers.

Their training was completed around April 17th 1918, and soon after this date the Engineers would make the trip to New York City, New York for their departure to the war in France. The Engineers were barracked in new facilities at Camp Merritt on the evening of April 28th. The unit was given passes to go to New York City and to see the City of Cities during their 24-hour pass.

On the morning of May 8th the unit steamed out of the New York harbor and passed the Statute of Liberty and proceeded to cross the Atlantic toward France. They landed at Brest Harbor in the morning of May 18th and were billeted at the Pontanezen Barracks where they spent several days repairing docks for railroad yardage and short periods of drills while awaiting transportation to the front lines.

The docks, yards and campsite at Brest were soon after developed by the American Expeditionary Forces into one of the most important ports serving our Army in Europe.
On the 24th of May the company made it's first meeting with the soldier's passenger service that they would embark on. They were loaded onto a string of railroad cars called "Forty and Eights", the cars are typical boxcars. The name "Forty and Eights" came from the inscriptions on the sides of the cars—"40 Hommes, 8 Chevaux," meaning forty men or eight horses to the car.

On May 25th they settled in some Prison Barracks, which were built originally for German Prisoners of War. On May 27th the Engineers began to clear land for building warehouses and railroad yards. On June 16th the Engineers moved their camp closer to the center of the work, and were living in some Hospital tents about a mile from the prison barracks. One of the best diversions that we had was to swim in the waters of the Cher River, about a mile from the camp.

We spent the next two months and seventeen days at Gievres, the site was a reclaimed swamp of approximately 2,000 acres of scattered brush and pine groves, which we had to clear out, and continued to build large complexes of warehouses, and yardages to take care of the large receipt, storage and distribution of large quantities of supplies needed for the war effort.

The Engineers cleared, drained and leveled the major portion of an area two and a half miles long, by three-eights of a mile wide. They graded the surfaces and laid about six and three-quarters of a mile of tracks and installed ten small bridges. They constructed two steel warehouses 504 by 50 feet, four frame warehouses 504 by 50 feet, and the housing of five Bakery buildings 120 by 60 feet, which had a production capacity of one million pounds of bread daily.

On July 14th, the French Independence Day, we had a very impressive ceremony and parade including the French Battalion at Romorantin. On Saturday, August 10th we were given orders to prepare to march to the front. Our tools, wagons, equipment and horses were loaded on cars that evening and in the following morning of August 11th, we were loaded on to the box cars in lots of 40, with the usual allotment of food and provisions. As we pulled out of our first permanent camp and looked at the vast expanse of warehouses with the network of railroad tracks and compared it with the scene of our arrival at Gievres, we would not refrain from the feeling of the proud work we had accomplished.

On August 11th we came to Bricon, Haute Marne, and detrained and camped out. We hiked for 15 miles that day into Ville Sous LaFerte. In this area the 318th Engineers merged with the Army's 6th Division. We had fifteen days of intensive training which meant many miles of hiking with full packs. We did some work on trenches and barbwire entanglements. We were billeted at French homes, with which we made many friends.

On August 20th we left Ville Sous LaFerte by trucks, stopping the next morning at Belle Fontaine. We spent three days camped on green slopes in pup tents and did some more training, such as hiking. We daily soaked our sore feet at cool streams at Belle Fontaine. Sunday, September 1st, we were reloaded in trucks bound for the Gerardmer Section on the Alsace front to relieve the 35th

Division. We then moved into the foothills of the Vosges Mountains and ended up at LeCollet, about 4 miles from the sector we would occupy.

Here was a Red Cross Canteen, Y Hut, First Aid Station and a small camp back in the woods. There was a mass of troops, artillery and trucks moving through this point, to and from the front. While we were waiting to be lined up an ammunition truck caught fire and soon was in flames. It was only small arms ammunition but as the shells began to explode and whistle through the air, our column was hurried forward in the darkness with a hazy suspicion that some air raid had caused the fire, and a confused feeling of doubt as to whether we were already at the front or just going.

We then proceeded to move out in the darkness through the steep trails of the Vosges Mountains. We were fully packed out and had to do much hiking in the mountains. When we were in close range of the artillery fire, and due to our tiredness made us immune to the strange unfriendly fire.

We were exhausted and hungry men that reached Camp Nicolas in the early morning of September 2nd. The camp was opposite the enemy front near Colmar and though provided with a good system of dug-outs, it was naturally defended from artillery fire by virtue of its position on the opposite slope of a steep mountain, among the large and thickly growing pine trees. In the lower gulches were thick growths of ripe blue berries, raspberries and blackberries; and in spite of the admonitions of the few remaining French soldiers, that we were inviting artillery fire, many cupfuls of berries were picked and eaten. These berries were a relief from the few days of straight canned hash, corn-willie and hard tack of our emergency rations.

This sector prior to 1918 had been bitterly contested piece of territory in which the French had lost about 20,000 men, advancing their lines across the rugged country to where they held the dominating positions along the most prominent crests. There were many wooden crosses along this sector, which bore the grim circumstances of their losses. At this sector could be seen many aeroplanes making their raiding parties to maintain the positions that were gained, and also could be seen the puffs of smoke from the anti-aircraft guns shooting at the planes.

The Company was divided into platoons, which had specific tasks to accomplish, namely digging trenches, operating a sawmill and stringing barbwire, camouflaging and other duties. A few were employed as runners to maintain liaison between the scattered platoons, the Company, and Battalion Headquarters, and others at the Tramway head, which was a necessary conveyance to the rough mountain country. The worst thing was to deal with the Pack and Wagon train in the distribution of rations. The latter was a real problem because of the nature of the terrain. Our diet consisted of carrots and canned soup, which had a concoction of miscellaneous chopped vegetables.

The chronic rainy season of France was setting in after our arrival at Alsace; while the chill of the fall air and cold nights already felt in the mountains, brought forth the first light snow of the season before our departure. One exception to this was the view of "No-Mans Land"; here was the main street of business, and no matter how dark or rainy the night, could be seen the persistent flares or the Roman candles and sky rockets flashing signals up and down the two opposing trenches, lighting up the space between, with the brightness of day to expose raiding parties or surprise attacks on the part of the enemy. As the skyrockets broke and hovered over No-Mans Land with the clatter of machine guns and explosions of heavy shells, you were often reminded of a weird sac- religious attempt at celebrating the fourth of July.

The seclusion of Camp Nicolas became a matter of uncertainty on Saturday night of September 28th, when raiding parties operated generally along the southwest sector adjacent to the camp. The artillery and machine gun fire was active most of the night in which the enemy attempted to repulse advances from that section of our trenches. A number of prisoners were taken with few casualties in our Infantry, and the demolished trenches required several days and nights work by the Company in restoring them to a place of safety.

Many of the Camps and roads in the Alsace were the targets of long established ranges by the enemy as could be seen from the accuracy with which they dropped the high explosive and gas shells, in their periodical attacks along this part of the front. We were generally protected or hidden by a well planned system of covered trenches, galleries, dug-outs and camouflaging; yet it was only a matter of good fortune the Company passed their 40 days there with the many close calls from bursting shells or snipers' rifles and escaped with only a few slight shrapnel wounds.

The first French Division relieved us on October 10th, and early in the morning of the 11th the Company was again together, hiking with full packs along there way south and west through Vosges from the Alsace sector. We had covered over 21 miles arriving at Kruth near the foothills of the mountains; where we pitched tents for the night and then hiking for 9 more miles the next day over steep mountainous roads into Bussang, Vosges.

After six weeks without seeing the sight of women, children or homes, we had a craving for sweet things, and we bought some grapes from the local stores. We remained at Bussang from October 12th to the 28th replacing clothing and undergoing daily inspections from individual fleet to Regimental; such time as we were not at Infantry drill or in battle formation charging some of the many knobs which rose so conveniently steep about the valley of Bussang.

Our outfit was loaded on Sunday evening of the 27th, that we again found ourselves late that night guests of the French box cars. The trip was short, and traveling back north and west into the Department of Marne where we were detrained at St. Menehould soon after daylight the next morning; and could we have but looked into the future 39 days, the trip would have seemed much shorter and altogether comfortable. Within these 39 days, the men equipped with heavy winter clothing, helmets, gas masks, rifles and full packs, were destined to hike approximately 313 miles through that sloppy desolated region of the Argonne forests toward the front near Sedan, and return to their training area in the Cote D'Or Department after the armistice.

It was at this time the Germans were making such rapid and general retreats, that no fixed front of positions could be identified; and when the rumors were so current concerning Austria's surrender and prospects of peace, although from here on we had no source of official news for many days.

Our first stop was made at Camp Besnier on the evening of October 29th, about 12 miles from St. Menehould. On our march this day, a short ways out of camp where we stopped for dinner, sheets of paper were seen fluttering from the sky lighting here and there along our way for several miles. Some of these were recovered during the stop for dinner and found to be German propaganda dropped in great numbers from aeroplanes. They were addressed in English, French and German disclaiming any responsibility for further prosecution of the war on the grounds that the Allied aims had been attained and the real people then representing the German Government, clamored for peace on the basis of the Allies' demands. While at Camp Besnier we began to see the most active part being carried out on the Air service, where flocks of 20 to 30 aeroplanes could be seen continually soaring in the air. On one occasion 89 were counted in one fleet emigrating toward the warmer districts of the front. It was here we listened to the last of that famous three-day barrage near Grand Pre, which did so much to wreck the remaining defenses of the enemy.

On November 1st we moved into the Argonne Forest across the shell-torn Hindenburg line, arriving late in the night at that water drenched salvage camp in the thick woods of the Argonne Forests; occupied for a few days before by the Germans. The first exclusive German Grave Yard was seen there just beyond our camp. On the morning of November 3rd we were dodging our way jerkily along the sloppy roads through the crowded masses of moving divisions. Apparently the most hard luck, but persevering class of traffic, was those of our schedule with the hobnails and heavy packs. From here on for many days we were to see only vast fields of shell holes, newly-made graves and skeletons of what not long ago had been villages sheltering and providing for the families of peaceful communities. Camp was pitched that night on a side hill near Fleaville, and after beginning work on some trenches the next morning we marched forward soon after noon in the direction of Grand Pre. We passed through that shattered town the same evening, November 4th, pitching our tents on the slope beyond. Mail was distributed from home about dark, and it was while the men were grouped about the few limited candlelight's in the pup tents, devouring news from home, that the air raid started. Lights were immediately extinguished and though most of us were already under the shelter-halves even there you felt strangely to the mercy of bombs and machine gun fire raining from the sky. The fire was aimed at the bridge into Grand Pre, and only a few casualties occurred. Around Grand Pre the Germans had made their most stubborn stands; and the bodies of dead Americans, French and German soldiers were every where, which told us the war was devastating to land and villages, the cost of war.

For a short distance the road was quite effectively blocked with fallen trees or craters caused by exploding shells; but further along the way along their retreat had become so urgent that the work was only partially done. On either side of the road large trees were only half fallen, with explosives already placed, or the disabled equipment, heavy guns, dead horses and men. This day's hike of about 21 miles with this work and scanty rations was probably our strongest test, and when we reached the side hill above Authe late at night. This one night stings the dullest of our memories into recalling how we groped about in the rain and darkness for a smooth place to lie down, where most of us spread the shelter-halves and blankets on the ground pulling our necks in out of the cold rain, only to have the water trickle under us and form into puddles. There was much movement of trucks and troops as they withdrew from the front lines taking with them the civilian personnel that the Germans had let go. We received daily rumors that the war was over and that the armistice for peach was forthcoming, and the probability that the 6th Division was being withdrawn.

After four days and nights in which we were working day and night improving conditions to restore the orderly movement of traffic, the 6th Division was ordered to the rear, and on November 10th Company D was on their return hike, pitching camp that night at the old site near Grand Pre. This time heavy frost was on the ground, and as the rest of the Regiment had arrived earlier, a corner of the field, which was filled with shell-holes and barbed wire entanglements, fell to our share. The next day we marched to Camp Cheherry, occupying some old German Billets; where we were serenaded by shots throughout the night, purported to be a celebration of the armistice.

The good news of the armistice were not confirmed until the following day on our march toward Montfaucon, when a Herald was thrown to us form a Y.M.C.A. automobile, with the glaring headlines, "THE WAR IS WON". We cheered on and in spite of the cold we were all thinking about home.

We arrived at Montfaucon in the afternoon of November 11th. The masses of barbed wire entanglements, demolished trenches, shell holes and graveyards showed a bitter struggle had been waged. The next day we hiked 21 miles to Verdun, the stronghold of all fortified cities. The enemy had left and with their leaving had damaged homes and buildings.

On the second day we arrived at Adaucourt where we spent three days removing mines, or repairing roads and policing up much of the area, which had been the scene of early advances on Verdun. Day after day could be seen thousands of English, French, Italian and Russian prisoners that the Germans released; they were struggling to get home.

On the evening of November 19th we marched to a point northwest of Etain were we camped. Here our orders took on definite steps. On November 20th we started our return hike of several hundred miles to the training area of LaForet, Cote D'Or. The first night brought us back to Verdun and successive days marched until December 3rd when we arrived at LaFeret Sur Aube—the scene of our training in August. During the night at LaFerte Sur Aube, 2 miles below Ville Sous Laferte—which was our home for a brief time four months before. Many of the troops visited for the evening with some French friends, who extended a hearty welcome at our return.

It was December 4th as we reached the French Barracks at Montigny, which will go down as one of our memorable shelters. We proceeded to march to Leuglay that was 8 miles away. But a short hike the next day found us at LaFeret on the morning of the 6th. The anticipation of going to a port of embarkation for the States within a short time probably did much to stimulate the men through the hardships of the latter part of this memorable march. A company canteen, with supplies through purchases from the Division Quartermaster, was opened at LaFeret and for the first time since our arrival in France we were able to satisfy our many desires on the line of sweet food.

Soon after Christmas our Company was split up into small details and scattered over the Divisional area to begin the systematic repair and maintenance of the damaged roads. The men were very anxious to learn when they would go home. During the months of March and April the majority of the Company was able to take 7 or 14-day leaves, visiting many attractive centers in France or visit relatives in England and Italy.

The company was assembled on April 9th at St. Broing where the Company Headquarters was located, and on

April 10th joined the Regiment to take part in the Divisonal review before General Pershing near Duesme. On April 12th and April 14th the Company was on board a convoy of trucks bound for Germany, and the Army of Occupation. We were unloaded from the trucks the same evening and the following morning we were loaded in American boxcars that had more space than the crowded French ones. The train moved out of Latrecey on April 15th taking us northwest via Verdun, Metz, across Lorraine, through Luxemborg and the German province of Rhine to Cochem, a short distance south of Cablenz. We were detrained shortly before noon April 16th, and hiked for 10 miles to Aldegund, were we billeted in German homes with feather beds and surprisingly good surroundings.
Our Division was relieving the 4th, and as a few troops were left behind for guard duty.
The Company established a guard at Aldegund on April 19th, and sent two platoons out to maintain guard at tunnels and railroad bridges. These platoons were relieved on April 30th when the Infantry arrived, but on May 3rd the third and fourth platoons were hiked to Bad Bertrich for further guard duty.
To our astonished pleasure preparations were at once put under way to leave. After the company was assembled toward exchange of equipment and clothing, salvaging wagons, and on May 16th all horses were turned in.
Physical inspections again became a daily occurrence, and the office was busy day and night classifying the men to their respective demobilization Camp for distribution to the States.
On May 24th we were transported by truck from Aldegund to Cochem, where we entrained in American boxcars enroute to Brest. It requires four nights and

three days to cover the distance from Germany to the extreme northwest part of France. Twelve hours were lost when we collided with a passenger train just beyond Tours. The only damage was to the coach that resulted in the delay. The train carried us via Trier, Germany, Etain, Abacourt, Verdun, and through French Departments of Meuse, Haute Marne, Aube, Yonne, Loiret, Loir Etcher, via Gievres, Tours, Lemans and Rennes, arriving at Brest on May 28th. Although this was the longest of our railroad trips in Europe, the knowledge of our destination and the assurance that it was to be our last boxcar tour of France, made it easier to take the 84 hours cooped up in the train until we detrained in Brest.

We hiked from the Brest railroad yards on the afternoon of May 28th over the road we had marched to Pontanzen Barracks in the same month a year ago. Since we had camped at Pontanzen, the American forces had built a large modern Camp, which could accommodate 100,000 troops during the course of preparing for embarkation.

A few minutes after reaching the Barracks we were put through a physical, then hurried through the de-lousing station and bathhouse. We then picked up new clothing. On the fourth day we again completed our physicals, de-lousing and baths.

On June 2nd we were ordered to roll packs for departure. We hiked down to the Brest wharf, checked out and marched on the Lighter that carried us to the S.S. Orizada. The Orizada was much smaller than the S.S. America on which we had crossed before, yet there were 4,000 troops and 410 sailors. The passage took eight days and on June 10th the lighthouse at Cape Henry of the most coveted land dimly appeared in the distance. The ship cast anchor on the Chesapeake Bay at Newport News, Virginia. From the stations of enlistment until our happy return to Newport News the Company had traveled by rail and water between twelve and thirteen thousand miles, and this did not count our land travel. With a band at the head of the column we marched from the pier to Camp Stuart, on the outskirts of Newport News. Along the line of marching that morning a strong welcome of shouts greeted us, and the schools along the route turned out with a chorus of yells and demonstration of patriotism.

As we look back over the part our Company played in making the American Expeditionary forces what they were, it is to feel pride and satisfaction in having done our best. The Company stood ever anxious and ready to face any angle of the game that the Americans were fighting with a force of spirit. That was new to the European warriors. No more capable and conscientious Company of 250 men were ever assembled for the duties that were theirs' and took up their work with a greater spirit of loyalty.

On June 18th, 1919 the Company was disbanded and mustered out of the United States Army to civilian life. Among them, off course was William Peterson, Jr., who was discharged on October 14, 1919.

Chapter 2   THE EVENTFUL YEARS

In the United States 1920 census taken on January 10th the family is living in a rented house on 5 Fugero Court in Easthampton, Massachusetts. Living with the family are William, Sr., Flora and children William, age 22, Lillian, age 16, Maude, age 14, and Fred W., age 4 years and six months. They also had living in their rented house a boarder, which was customary in that time period to make ends meet. William, Sr, and William, Jr., were both working as laborers for a contractor. Lillian is listed as working for a woolen mill as a spinner and sister Maude working at the woolen mill as a hand. Also in the United States 1920 census finds Isabelle Seymour living at Hill Avenue in Easthampton, Massachusetts. She is living with Tuffield Pete and his wife Gertrude. Tuffield is William Pete's Sr, brother. Four days after the census was taken Isabelle Seymour and William, Jr. are married on June 14, 1920. Note that William's surname reverts back to Pete from Peterson. The marriage certificate shows William as a mechanic and Isabelle as a mill operator. The groom's parents are listed as William Pete and Flora Bottom, and the bride's parents are listed as George Seymour and Alma St. Anthony. The official of the marriage is Reverend J. F. Bourasse.

The United States Census of 1930 shows William Peterson, Sr., and his wife Flora living on a farm in East Granby, Connecticut. Both William and Flora were 19 and 15 when first married. Both William and Flora were both from New York, and the three children living with them were born in Connecticut. However, William was actually born in Massachusetts. William changed his surname from Pete to Peterson probably in the 1920's.

The United States Census of 1930 lists William Peterson, Jr., and his wife Isabelle and their children residing at 28 Second Street, Hartford, Connecticut. The children listed are: Loretta, age 10, William G., age 9, Arthur, age 9, both William and Arthur were born in the same year, William in January and Arthur in December, Lawrence, age 7, Henry (Hank), age 5, Donald, age 3, Dorothy, age 1, and Barbara age 1 month old. William was working as a truck driver.

William apparently is having difficulties supporting such a large family, and to keep his identity secret he added an additional "t" to his surname, and Peterson became Petterson. This change to his surname made it most difficult to find him and his family in 1930. Most of the problems of the large family were primarily due to the Great Depression. Many families during this grave time period ran into financial difficulties. It was devastating to the families of that era; so drastic measures were to be taken whether good or bad. In the case of William's family it was indeed very bad. In 1933 the living conditions became so bad that the State of Connecticut stepped in and made six of the children wards of the State.

Henry (Hank) Peterson remembers that while on the farm of William, Sr. in 1933 he saw a brand new 1933, black Cadillac in the garage with chickens running all over it. It is unknown how the Caddy was purchased; however, it is assumed that William, Jr., purchased it with the proceeds from sale of bootlegged liquor, as he was a bootlegger during that time frame. The Cadillac never left the garage probably because William, Sr., was embarrassed or that seeing it might draw suspicion to some kind of illegal acts at the farm.

The children were taken by the State and placed in the Hartford County Home located at Warehouse Point, Connecticut. Jane was born a month after the children were taken to the home. At this point in time there were ten children and Raymond was to be born in 1934 making a total of eleven children.

In 1935 the five boys were transferred to Mount St. John's School in Deep River, Connecticut. Loretta was assigned to a foster home in 1935 in Hartford, Connecticut. In 1938, the State of Connecticut was placing the rest of the children in foster homes. Arthur went to Simsbury, Connecticut, Lawrence went to Hartford, Connecticut, William, Donald and Henry went to Plantsville, Connecticut.

In 1941 Arthur enlisted in the U.S. Army in the Infantry as World War 2 had just started with the involvement of the United States. Lawrence enlisted in the Navy in 1942; this is when he finds out that his real first name is Andrew. William also went into the Navy in 1942. Henry enlisted in the Navy in 1943, and Donald enlisted in 1945, he also found out his real first name was Robert. William was stationed in an aircraft carrier, Andrew was stationed on a destroyer, Henry was in the Navy Armed guard, and Robert was in the Seebees. All of the brothers came home safely after the war had ended, and all obtained honorable discharges and were sent to civilian life.

In the mean time, William, Jr., left his wife Isabelle in Hartford, Connecticut to fend for her self and the remaining children. He did come back to move Isabelle to Massachusetts at a later date.

 Barbara who born in late 1929 was adopted by Albina (Pete) Boucher and her husband in 1930, she is the daughter of Peter Pete and Leizida Pete, Peter Pete was the grandson of Pierre Pitre and Marie Louise Reaume. The children who remained at home with Isabelle were: Jane, Dorothy, Jimmy and Raymond.

William Peterson surfaces in Lowell, Massachusetts in about 1934. William Peterson, now William Donovan marries Vera Caroline Nowak on October 13, 1934. On the marriage certificate the groom is listed, as William L. Donovan and the bride as Vera Caroline Nowak. William lists his age as 33 and Vera lists her age as 24. William is employed as a machinist, and Vera is employed at a mill operator. William lists his birthplace as Salt Lake City, Utah, and Vera lists Lowell, Massachusetts as her birthplace. The parents of William are William Donovan and Flora E. Buttena, (notice that William has changed the maiden name of his mother from Bottom to Buttena.) He also changed the surname of his father from Peterson to Donovan. This becomes William's second marriage. The parents of Vera are John Nowak and Catherine Nostek, and listed for both is their first marriage. They were married at the Polish Orthodox Church located on 1938 Lakeview Avenue, Lowell, Massachusetts, and married by L. A. Ciesinski, Priest. The marriage announcement is listed as follows: Miss Vera Caroline Nowak, daughter of Mr. and Mrs. John Nowak of Dracut and Mr. William L. Donovan son of Mr. William L. Donovan of 37 Hanover street (the parents actually lived in East Granby, Connecticut, the Hanover address was a boarding house) will be married at 4 o'clock this afternoon in Holy Trinity church by Rev. Ciesinski, Priest. The couple will be attended by Miss Stella Rita Nowak, a sister of the bride, as maid of honor and Mr. Joseph Szafran as best man. This announcement appeared in the Lowell Courier-Citizen, Saturday, October 13, 1934.

Miss Nowak will wear a white satin wedding gown with train and shoulder length veil and will carry a bouquet of bridal roses and lilies of the valley. Her attendant will be dressed in peach taffeta with a green velvet turban and accessories to match and will carry Talisman roses.

Immediately after the ceremony a reception will be held at the bride's home 93 Clark Avenue, Dracut. The couple will leave on a wedding trip to Connecticut. Miss Nowak is a graduate of St. Patrick's and Lowell High Schools, while Mr. Donovan attended school in Simsbury, Conn. and Williston Academy. William left Vera in Hartford, Connecticut to fend for her self for a couple of years, as he decided to travel on his own. While in Hartford William gives Vera One Thousand Dollars that he received for his invention on the automatic screw machine, probably when he worked at C. G. Sargents and Sons in Graniteville, Massachusetts some time ago.

Ironically, Isabelle's last child Raymond fathered by William on October 8, 1934, just five days before William married Vera Nowak.

William and Vera resided at 538 Bridge Street, in Lowell, Massachusetts. William worked for C. G. Sargents from January 1935 to November 1937. William's mother Flora LaFond passes on May 14, 1936 at East Granby, Connecticut. She dies from a heart attack. Here is what the obituary states: The funeral of Mrs. Flora Peterson, wife of William Peterson of Tunxis Street, was largely attended Monday morning at St. Bernard's church where the Rev. James H. Grady, Pastor, was the celebrant of a Requiem High Mass for there repose of her soul. Mrs. Peterson died suddenly last Thursday of a heart ailment.

During the Mass, Mathew J. Leach, organist rendered De Profundis at the offertory and "Tenderly and Sweet Jesus is Calling" at the conclusion. Internment took place in the family plot in St. Bernard's cemetery, where Father Grady read the committal service. The bearers were Frank Wall, Martin Norkitis, (Martin was boyfriend of Maude Peterson, who passed away in 1949), Peter Peterson, Henry Lamontin, Edward Turcott and Albert Tetreault. Mrs. Peterson is survived by her husband, two married daughters and two sons Henry and Russell of Tariffville. Notice that William Lawrence Peterson, Jr. was not mentioned in the obituary. Also, Fred Peterson was not mentioned. The obituary was reported in The Farmington Valley Herald on Thursday, May 21, 1936.

On November 7, 1937 at the time of his son John Lawrence Donovan's birth at Lowell, Massachusetts he listed his name as William L. Donovan, and that he was born in Salt Lake City, Utah in 1897. My mother told me that when William saw his child John, he exclaimed, "What is that"!

On the Social Security form SS-5, Application for Social Security Account Number, (The Act became law in 1935); he lists his name as William Lawrence Donovan, residing at 538 Bridge Street, Lowell, and Massachusetts. He is listed as working for C.G. Sargents Sons Corp. on Broadway in Graniteville, Massachusetts. His date of birth was listed as August 16, 1897, place of birth Salt Lake City, Utah. His father is listed as William L. Donovan and his mother as Flora Bottomley. This time he changes his father's surname from Peterson to Donovan, and his mother's maiden name to Bottomley from Bottom. The document is signed on December 1, 1936. Two more children are born to William and Vera, Patricia Carol Donovan on July

11th 1939 and Gail Lorraine Donovan on January 27, 1942 in Lowell, Massachusetts. Both now reside in Seymour and Stratford, Connecticut respectively.

Chapter 3 THE ADVENTUROUS YEARS

Now the adventure of a lifetime starts for William Donovan, AKA Peterson. William decides to go to California to find work in Oakland. The family of Vera and son John go with him to seek employment in California. Upon arrival in California William goes to work for the Palmer Chase Company, in Oakland, California. He works there from early March 1939 through early July of 1939. This is where Patricia Carol Donovan is born on July 11, 1939 in Oakland, California on Trenor Street that later becomes McArthur Blvd. William does not provide funds for his wife Vera to run the household, and when Patricia was born there was no money to pay for the doctor delivering Patricia; to this day there is no birth certificate for Patricia, the doctor never provided one, probably because he was not paid. William decides to venture back to Massachusetts after his short employ in California.

While on the trip back to Massachusetts, Patricia gets ill. William drives to Salt Lake City, Utah and receives medical aid for Patricia from the Mormon Church in Salt Lake City. Upon arrival in Massachusetts, William obtains employment with the Atlantic Rayon Corp. of Massachusetts located in Lowell. After a short stay there he again goes back to work for C. G. Sargents Sons in Graniteville, Massachusetts. He and his family are residing at 538 Bridge Street, Lowell, Massachusetts. He works there from October 1939 to March 1940. By March 1940 William worked for the Wikstrom Realty Corp. in Roslindale, Massachusetts from late March through mid-June 1940. After even a shorter term of employment with them he works for Waltham Industries Corp. & Subsidiaries in Waltham, Massachusetts from late June through mid-July 1940. We believe that William stayed in the New England area.

(Note: Job positions are based on Social Security Records. There are instances when the home office of the company that William was reported working for was not necessarily the same location as the job site. Each of these reported positions and actual work locations would have to be reviewed separately for accuracy. This has been done for most of the jobs.) Meanwhile, the family, Vera, John and Patricia are residing with Vera's mother and the children's grandparents at 93 Clark Avenue, Dracut, Massachusetts later to become 75 Clark Avenue. After a short tenure at Waltham Industries William works at the Woonsocket, Rhode Island plant of Taft-Peirce Manufacturing Company of Bellwood, Illinois, which is a small town just west of Chicago in Cook County. William worked for the company from July through mid-December 1940. By late 1940 William was working for Lombard Industries, Inc., in Ashland, Massachusetts until June 1941. From July 1941 through late February 1942 William worked for the Franklin Machine & Foundry Company in Providence, Rhode Island.

The family moved from Dracut, Massachusetts to go to Woonsocket, Rhode Island in 1941 and resided at 2320 Diamond Hill Road in that city. I remember being there, as I took walks down to the ice cream parlor, I also remember being stung by a swarm of hornets. William followed this employment with a short stay with Automatic Machine Manufacturing Company in Bridgeport, Connecticut from February through early April 1942, and even a shorter stay in May 1942 at W. H. Nichols & Sons in Waltham, Massachusetts. In late April he took a position with Bullard Company of Bridgeport, Connecticut, which lasted until August 1942.

Gail Lorraine Donovan was born on January 27, 1942 in Lowell, Massachusetts; the family was residing at 93 Clark Avenue, Dracut, Massachusetts with Vera's parents and the children's grandparents. After Bullard, William took employment with Middlesex Village Motor Company in Lowell, Massachusetts from April through November 1942. Still in the New England area William started employment with Manning, Maxwell & Moore, Inc., located in the Chrysler Building in New York City, New York. He would work in their Manchester, New Hampshire plant until early May of 1943. His wife Vera would accompany him in Manchester for that period. The children would stay in Dracut.

William took a position in late May 1943 with United Technologies Corporation in Hartford, Connecticut, which is a company later on to be known as Sikorsky's Aircraft where he worked for the firm until July 1943 (William became a friend of Igor Sikorsky, the helicopter pioneer) before taking a short-term employment with Laurias Machine Company, also in Hartford from July through August 1943.

Late in August 1943 William found employment with Northam Warren Company in Stamford, Connecticut where he was employed until mid March 1944. Once again, William found a succession of short-term employments, working for Healey Investment Company of Stamford, Connecticut from late March through June 1944, and then working for the Singer Company of San Leandro, California in their Business Machines Division in Bridgeport, Connecticut in July 1944. He also worked for a short period of time at the Hershey Metal Products

Company of Derby, Connecticut from September through December of 1944.

Enter the post-war era; the Federal Electric Products Company in Newark, New Jersey through July 1945 employs William. In August, William started working for the Greist Manufacturing Company in New Haven, Connecticut. There is no record of any earnings for William from October through December 1946. His employment records resume with Greist Manufacturing Company in January 1947 through May 1947 when he returned to work for Hershey Metal Products Company in Derby, Connecticut from May through November 1947.

I do remember going to see dad at the Derby plant of the Hershey Metals Products Company. The family is now residing at 365 Ruth Street, Bridgeport, Connecticut in an owned home. Son John resided with the family for a short period of time and returned to Dracut, Massachusetts because Vera could not take care of three children at one time. Son John would stay in Dracut, except for some short stays in Connecticut until he graduated from grammar school at the Parker Avenue Junior High School in 1951, at Dracut, Massachusetts.

William becomes restless again and both 1948 and 1949 appear to have been lean years for him. He began to travel again and was not as readily able to move from position to position leaving gaps in his reported earnings. William began the year working at the Hershey Metal Products Company in Ansonia, Connecticut where he was employed until the first week of April. He seems to have been without work for a while after this position, reporting only about a week of employment at the Waterbury, Connecticut plant of Beverwyck Breweries, Inc. of Albany, New York sometime between July and September 1948. He then reported working for about two or three weeks between October and December 1948 at the new Haven, Connecticut plant of Kerlikon Motch Corporation of Cleveland, Ohio.

In February 1949, William is working at Charles Fischer Spring Company in New York, New York, where he remained until June of the same year. He then worked for two or three weeks at the Kaman Corporation in Bloomfield, Connecticut in July or August 1949, and for about one week, likely in September 1949 at Norwich, Connecticut plant of Cleminshaw & Cleminshaw, a Division of the J. M. Cleminshaw Company in Cleveland, Ohio. His position in 1949 was reported with the Matson Mill, Inc. in Wakefield, Rhode Island where he worked for about two weeks sometime in November or December 1949. Between the years of 1946 and 1947 William left his second wife, Vera and family, only to be seen sporadically in the future until 1961 which was the last contact with William by this family. Starting in 1950 William is employed by the Johns Hartford Tool Company, Inc., in Newington, Connecticut from mid January through March 1950, and he could be found during working hours at Hartford Lumber Company in Hartford, Connecticut in April of that year. In May 1950 William was working the Emhart Manufacturing Company in Hartford, Connecticut, where he enjoyed employment until late January 1951. William was on the move in 1951, finding employment at the Bridgeport, Connecticut plant of Olivetti Corporation of Tarrytown, New York from early February through mid August of that year. However, in late August William returned to Massachusetts and was working for Precision Engineering Company of Springfield, Massachusetts. He worked for that company until mid March of 1952.

By this time wife Vera, daughters, Patricia and Gail as well as son John were living on 232 French Street, Bridgeport, Connecticut. The family is on State aid at this point and life was most difficult. John had joined the family after June 1951. Vera's mother, Katharina (Nostek) Nowak passed in July 29, 1951 from heart problems. In the same year on July 12, 1951, William Peterson, Sr. passed in Hartford, Connecticut also from a heart condition. The obituary on William Peterson, Sr., reads as follows: William Peterson of Granby, Connecticut died at Hartford Hospital, July 12, 1951. Mr. Peterson is survived by one daughter; Mrs. Elberta Chatfield of Granby; four sons, Lawrence R. Peterson of Hazardville, Henry E. Peterson of Bloomfield, Fred J. Peterson of Hartford, and William L. Peterson of Washington, D. C.; two sisters, Mrs. Gilbert of Morris, New York, and Mrs. Elizabeth Seymour of Stonington; one brother, Peter Peterson of Holyoak, Mass.; and four grandchildren. Funeral services were held from Charles H. Vincent and Sons Funeral Home, Simsbury, with requiem mass at St. Bernard's Church, Tariffville, Monday, July 17. Burial was in St. Bernard's cemetery, Tariffville.

William came to the home of Vera and children during that time frame and stayed only for a few hours, and is gone again. He gave me a quarter, I begged him to stay, but he left. In 1952 sister Carol says that William came to the house on 232 French Street, Bridgeport, Connecticut and picked her up and they went to Hartford where William bought Carol some clothes, including a bathing suit. They then went to some ladies apartment in West Hartford, but she was not at home so they spent the night in Hartford and later went to visit William's sister Lillian (Babe) also known as Elberta and her husband

Elmer. William left Carol there for a couple of days and then from there they went to visit his brother Russell and wife Jean in Hazardville, and stayed there for two days and nights. Carol thinks that William was trying to find a place for her to stay.

In the later part of March of 1952 found William working for a short time for Ace Tool and Design Company in Hartford, Connecticut before he started working with Taag, Inc., of Cambridge, Massachusetts. He worked for Taag from February through early May of 1952. Mid to late May 1952 found William working for the Marc A. Porter Company in Newington, Connecticut, where he stayed through mid August. He finished 1952 by working at the Bridgeport, Connecticut facilities of National Crown Engineering & Manufacturing Corp., Inc. of Philadelphia, Pennsylvania, where he was employed from mid August through April 1953, and from January through April, 1954 William worked for Electric Indicator Company, Inc., in Norwalk, Connecticut. According to the employment records he was not working from April 1954 through October 1955, where he worked for Arron Hydraulic Manufacturing Company in East Hartford, Connecticut until the first week of January 1956.

William during the period 1955 and 1956 meets his fourth wife to be, Marjorie Hecht. The meeting came about when William was working on one of his inventions and needed someone to draft his drawings. Someone recommended Marjorie Hecht, who worked at the Kaman Corporation in Bloomfield, Connecticut to do the work for William. He took his work to Marjorie's apartment in West Hartford and she did his drawings. Sometime in 1955 and 1956 William is romancing Marjorie Hecht and is visiting her in West Hartford, Connecticut on a regular basis, and continues to romance Marjorie even when he goes to work at the Portsmouth Naval Shipping Yards in Portsmouth, New Hampshire. He commutes back and forth from there to West Hartford, Connecticut where Marjorie resided.

Son John graduates as an honor student from Central High School, Bridgeport, Connecticut on June 8th 1955 and attends Boston University and the Hartford Institute of Accounting during 1955 and 1956.

William comes to pick up Carol in 1955 on her 16th birthday, which is on July 11th; he buys her a record player and other gifts. They both went to Agnes Hael Southworth's home in East Granby, Connecticut and threw a party for Carol. Carol stayed there for a week and William takes her back home.

It is not known if William was self-employed or acting as a consultant during these unemployed periods, or if he was actually out of work. The Social Security Administration did not require self-employed individuals to participate in the Social Security program. Self-employed individuals could opt to not participate in the program.

In February and March of 1956 William worked for the Delta Corporation in East Granby, Connecticut. At this period of time is when William showed up at the family rent subsidized government residence at 512 Harral Avenue, Bridgeport, Connecticut and asked his wife Vera for a divorce. However, Vera being a Catholic did not grant him his wish. I remember when he came to Bridgeport, Connecticut at this time frame, and I remember seeing him in his brand new 1957 Nash. He then proceeded to marry Agnes Hael Southworth in Hartford, Connecticut in 1956. Jean Peterson, wife of Russell Peterson, brother of William Peterson, AKA Donovan, who attended the marriage, has substantiated this marriage and the reception held at Agnes's home in East Granby, Connecticut. Also, Donald Peterson, son of one of William's brothers, who visited the newlywed couple at Pompano Beach, Florida in 1956, also provided proof of the marriage. Donald also remembers seeing William's latest inventions at the home.

Also, during Thanksgiving Day of 1957 William picked up Carol and they went to Agnes's home in East Granby, Connecticut (she also had the home in Pompano Beach, Florida), and proceeded to visit William's brother Russell in Hazardville, Connecticut as well as Russell's wife Jean Nolan and brother Henry and one other brother, which Carol did not remember. William returned Carol to 512 Harral Avenue after the visits. William shortly thereafter left Agnes, his third wife and started to travel again.

William worked for Kay Nash Motors, Inc., in Ft. Lauderdale, Florida for a few weeks in the first quarter of 1957. Apart from those two jobs, William reported wages when he worked at Carts Incorporated in Pompano Beach, Florida for about one week in the fourth quarter of 1957. The Social Security Administration listed no other reportable earnings for this time period.

Agnes Hael Southworth Donovan's death certificate in 1985 lists Agnes as widowed. Since William died in 1982 this is accurate. Agnes's first husband's brother, Robert Southworth was still living nearby in Florida. He signed as the informant on her death certificate. He also arranged for her body to be moved to Rocky Hill, Connecticut for burial. Agnes's sister, Anne Murray is also buried in the same cemetery. Agnes's first husband was Albert Southworth, Albert Southworth died in October of 1967 in Hartford, Connecticut, he was born

December 26, 1898. Albert and Agnes had two children born to them. Albert and Agnes Hael Southworth appeared in the Hartford City Directory in 1930, which showed her as residing in East Granby, Connecticut.

1958 did not start out much better for William. He worked for about one or two weeks in the third quarter for Universal Design, Inc., of Hartford, Connecticut, possibly in August or September upon his arrival from Florida. In mid-November, however, he began employment at the Middlebury, Connecticut plant of Precision Industrial Design Company, Inc., of Nutley, New Jersey where he stayed until June 1959. From July 1959 through March 1960 no income was reported for William, until he started working for Vector Engineering, Inc., of Rockville, Maryland. William would work for this company numerous times over the next few years. This employment lasted until September 1960, with no earnings reported for the remainder of 1960.

In 1961 William calls Vera; Carol who was baby-sitting at the time at another location was called by Vera and said that William wants her to go with him and to live with him permanently. Carol says no and that is the last time Carol or anyone in our family ever heard from him again. Several years later in 1971 Carol inquires to Aunt Lillian "Babe" about the whereabouts of William and Babe said he was the mayor of Tombstone, Arizona, which Carol did not pursue this. A later check with Tombstone showed that William was not the mayor of Tombstone. Ironically, William and Marjorie Hecht were only forty miles from Tombstone in the direction of Dragoon, Arizona.

William would return to the Portsmouth Naval Shipping Yards working for Atlantic Designs Company many times through 1967. William completed a small, perhaps one or two week period for Vector in the first quarter of 1961 before moving on to Bartone & Lawrence Paramount Designs, Inc., in Brooklyn, New York, where he worked from April through mid June 1961. He worked on another small one-week project for Independent Unions of New Jersey, in Newark, New Jersey in April 1961 before he started working at the Portsmouth Naval Shipping Yard in Portsmouth, New Hampshire for the Atlantic Design Company of Newark, New Jersey. He worked for Atlantic from July through November 1961 before changing his employment in December 1961 to work for Coastal Publications Corporation, in New York City, New York. William returned to the Portsmouth Naval Shipping Yards working for Atlantic Designs Company many times through 1967.

During this time frame he decided to marry Marjorie Hecht and married her as his fourth wife on May 16, 1966 at Virginia Beach, Virginia. The marriage certificate lists the groom as William Patrick Donovan; note the change in the middle name, which was Lawrence prior to his marriage. The bride lists her name as Marjorie Hecht. William lists himself as divorced, which off course is not correct, and Marjorie lists herself as single. By the way, Marjorie asked William if he finally got his divorce, and William said he did. Off course, he did not get the divorce from any of his wives.

Both William and Marjorie list their occupations as Engineers. William lists his birthplace as Ludlow, Massachusetts, and Marjorie lists her birthplace as New York City, New York.

William lists his mother as Mary Edna Bottom and father as William Patrick Donovan; Marjorie lists her mother as Natalie Happ, and father as Charles Henry Clay Hecht.

Note that William listed his mother's maiden name as Mary Edna Bottom, which is correct. William lists his address as 99 Row Street in Portsmouth, New Hampshire, and Marjorie lists her address as 1014 Trout Brook Drive, West Hartford, Connecticut. He and Marjorie resided on Becket Road, Otis, Massachusetts from 1966 through 1971 at a home that William and Marjorie purchased.

In 1962 William had not much work. He reports no earnings for the first quarter through mid June, when he worked for Consultants & Designers, Inc., in New York City, New York until mid July of that year. In July of 1962 William returned to work for Vector Engineering, Inc., of Rockville, Maryland, where he remained until April of 1963.

William became eligible for Social Security Benefits in 1962. This could explain the sparse employment he took. Yet, he would have been penalized for his heavier earnings from 1963 through 1968 if he had retired at either age 62 or age 65. It is more likely he restricted himself to selected projects and retired after 1968.

In April of 1963 William returned to the employ of Atlantic Designs Company of Newark, New Jersey working at the Portsmouth Naval Shipyard, Portsmouth, New Hampshire where he was employed until September of that year. In this year is when the accident on the submarine Thresher occurred; also in this time period Marjorie introduced William to Elizabeth Lewin, who was the niece of Marjorie's. Marjorie was concerned that William might have been on the USN Submarine Thresher when it went down on April 10, 1963; however William was scheduled for another shift on the Thresher and thus avoided the accident. William worked again for Atlantic Designs from January through

June 1964, and from January through June 1965. No earnings are reported for the third quarter of 1965, nor any earnings reported for July through December of both 1964 and 1965.

In 1966, Atlantic Designs Company could claim to be the longest-term employer for William. He worked again for the company from January through September of 1966, and then again from February through August 1967, where he was living with his fourth wife, Marjorie in their home in Otis, Massachusetts, Marjorie continued to work at Kaman Corporation of Bloomfield, Connecticut until her retirement in 1971. As of November through December 1967 William is reported working for Dynamic, Inc. in Marlboro, Massachusetts. He after that takes a short employment with Star Design, Inc., in Moorestown, New Jersey from March through June of 1968. At the end of December of 1968 William started what would be his last employment of record. He went to work for Dornado Corporation in Manchester, Connecticut where he remained in their employ until July of 1969.

Chapter 4   THE RETIREMENT YEARS

William retired at the end of 1969 and Marjorie retired in 1970, which is an early retirement at 62 for her. Marjorie's niece, Elizabeth Lewin, visited William and Marjorie frequently at Otis, Massachusetts. William and Marjorie added a new kitchen at the home and Marjorie decorated the kitchen and the rest of the home. Marjorie had been an interior designer during the 1930's and had a wonderful flare for home decorating. William would take Elizabeth's children fishing when they visited and the children loved it.

Residence records from family members indicate that William moved temporarily to Tucson, Arizona with his wife Marjorie in 1971 at the age of 71, they would spend two winters in Tucson and decided to sell their home in Otis, Massachusetts and to permanently live in Arizona. They purchased a home in Dragoon, Arizona on Second Street. They then proceeded to pick up their furniture in Otis, Massachusetts during 1972; they stopped at Elizabeth's home in Westport, Connecticut on the way to Dragoon, Arizona. Upon arrival in February 1972 they moved into their new home.

William constructed a workshop at the residence and did his tinkering, and inventions that he was working on. William developed a water purification system, as the water in Dragoon was poor. Everyone in the neighborhood wanted the system. He also built his own solar panels and installed them in his home; the system was used to heat the hot water.

One thing about William in his early years was that he drank liquor to excess, and he continued this practice in Dragoon. He would socialize with the neighbors on a daily basis and would be drinking liquor on the same basis, plus a lot of home cooking. Marjorie was an excellent cook and they both ate well as well as did some of the neighbors with them. William owned a pickup truck that he called "Lulabelle"; he loved that truck and Marjorie would know when William was coming home, because he honked as he approached the house.

Marjorie was sick several times and had to go to Tucson for medical assistance, which was 80 miles one-way. Marjorie and William, after she saw the doctor would go to a swank restaurant and have dinner. Marjorie is hospitalized several times and almost died after a surgery. William and Marjorie kept close contact with Marjorie's family in these trying times.

A friend of Elizabeth's, Loraine Wallace moved to Tucson, Arizona in 1978 and would visit Marjorie and William frequently and they would visit Loraine in Tucson also frequently. They all had a good time drinking and going to 5-star restaurant for dinners. Loraine Wallace gave an account of spending a lot of time with William and Marjorie; once they all went to a western hootenanny and drank heavily and went to a 5 star restaurant for dinner. There was also a time when they all went to a rodeo and ended in the same manner as above. Loraine stated that William and Marjorie had no or little money to spend so she gave them a fifty-dollar bill, as they were short. I must interject that every time I saw father that he had a roll of hundred dollar bills and was not broke, but this was in the 1940's, although Jean Peterson once said that William was always asking for money to further his inventions, but Jean and husband Russell never gave him any money. An attempt to get more information about William and Marjorie from Loraine failed. She kept a daybook on every thing that happened to her and her escapades; however she stopped giving me more information.

Marjorie had gotten pretty mad at William as he still would be a womanizer, even at his age and paid visits to the widowed ladies in the area.

Elizabeth visits William and Marjorie in January 1980 and spent time with Loraine in Tucson, as well spending time in Dragoon with William and Marjorie visiting places of interest. They went to Old Mexico across from Douglas, Arizona to Agua Prieta where William and Marjorie would purchase their liquor. William would also get his hair cut there. Again they would visit the fancy restaurants in Old Mexico, and have dinner, this was a special day and outing for both of them.

Elizabeth's son, Eric visited William and Marjorie in 1980. He went to Tucson for a visit to a friend, and then onto Dragoon to visit William and Marjorie. He would drink martinis with both of them and made a trip to Agua Prieta, Mexico. Coming back from Mexico at the border crossing the border agent asked how much liquor they were bringing into the United States, and William said that they had so much. The border agent just waved them through without checking the amount of liquor they actually possessed, which was a greater amount then he mentioned to the agent. During their retirement years William and Marjorie enjoyed a good time. However, Marjorie never did like Arizona and soon after William's death she would go to Iowa City, Iowa where her niece Natalie lived. She moved to Stamford, Connecticut when her niece relocated to Westchester, New York.

Marjorie Donovan signed William's death certificate on November 16, 1982. William died on November 14, 1982.

On William's death certificate his birth date is listed as August 16, 1900, and that he was born in Massachusetts. His occupation is listed as an engineer. The certificate lists his father as William Donovan, and his mother as Ann LaFond. Also listed is that he served in the United States military. William had suffered an arterial thrombosis and was admitted to the Tucson Medical Center on November 11, 1982. He died three days later. Marjorie died September 2, 2000 at the age of 92 in Stamford, Connecticut.

Chapter 5   CHILDREN AND WIVES

Let us now see how the children faired. Loretta Peterson married William Kimmel after the World War 2. He was a sergeant in the United States Army. They had three children, William, Steven and Lynn. The family settled in Millbury, Massachusetts.

Arthur Peterson was discharged from the United States Army in 1945 and married Katherine Sfakianos. They had three children, Robert, Linda and Cindy. Cindy died young at the age of nineteen from leukemia. Arthur was awarded the Silver Star for his service in 1944 for gallantry in action. He and two other soldiers were dropped off by submarine onto a Japanese fortified island and went ashore to map out the Japanese gun emplacements. They stayed on the island for three days hiding in the swamps to avoid the Japanese patrols and worked by nightfall to map the gun emplacements. They were picked up by submarine. Later, the United States invaded and took over the island from the Japanese. The ironic thing about Arthur Peterson receiving the Silver Star was that it wasn't awarded until 1993 by then President Clinton. Arthur Peterson and President Clinton appeared on the front page of the Telegram and Gazette, Worcester, Massachusetts. Arthur had petitioned Senator John Kerry sometime before receiving the medal and Senator Kerry petitioned President Clinton who then awarded the medal to Arthur. Arthur had said that he waited 48 years for the medal and that he knew he would have to go to the top to get his deserved medal.

William Peterson was discharged from the United States Navy in 1945 and in the same year he married June Lafgren. They had four children, Jan, William, Keith and

Susan. William served on the U.S. Princeton, an aircraft carrier that was sunk by the Japanese during the war in the battle of Leyte. He received the Purple Heart for wounds he sustained in the battle. He settled in Burlington, Connecticut. William remembers hearing from others that William, the father, worked on the bridge over the Connecticut River at Middletown, Connecticut. He also heard from others that he was working at the Terry Corporation in Windsor, Connecticut, and had a girl friend in West Hartford, Connecticut at Trout Brook Road.

Aunt Lillian (Babe) would take William out carousing on weekends leaving Isabelle at home with the children. While living in Windsor, Connecticut William would leave Isabelle with no food in the house. There was a woman who owned a small Italian store near her and she would give them food every night to exist on. The lady said that Aunt Irene, Fred's wife (he is the brother of William) used to give her William's information on his whereabouts, but because Fred Peterson passed on and Irene remarried and since they did not know where she lived all information was now gone.

Lawrence Peterson was discharged from the United States Navy in 1945. He met a lady from New York, by the name of Jane Tobin. They had three children, Sandra, Lawrence, and Robin. They settled in New York, New York, and then later to California, and eventually they married. Lawrence divorced and remarried in California to Dorothy and had four more children, Andrew, Mathew, Isabelle and Catherine.

Henry (Hank) Peterson was discharged from the United States Navy in 1946, where he served in the Armed Guard. He was involved in three invasions: Anzio, Selerno and Southern France. He received three battle stars for his service. He married in 1950 to Eileen Murphy. They had one child, Michael in 1951. They settled in Grafton, Massachusetts.

Robert Peterson was discharged from the United States Navy in 1946 and married a Millbury, Massachusetts's lady by the name of Theresa St. John. They had three children, Donna, David and Richard. They settled in Millbury, Massachusetts and many years later they moved to California.

Robert Peterson served with the United States Navy as a Seebee. He was stationed in Sipan, building airfields for the B-29's and B-26's, that used the base as a stop over to Tokyo.

James Peterson enlisted in the United States Army in 1951 during the Korean conflict, and spent time in Korea during that war. He met a woman in 1955 and later married her and had one child, Bruce. After a few years of marriage they were divorced. James saw a lot of action while in Korea; he was awarded the Bronze Star for bravery in action.

Raymond Peterson enlisted in the United States Navy in 1952. He served aboard a ship in the Atlantic. Raymond married in the 1950's, his marriage did not last very long and they were divorced a year later. He then moved to California. Raymond remarried in California to a lady named Martha; they separated for a while, but were living together when Raymond passed away in Arizona.

Dorothy Peterson, who later found out her real first name, was Ruth. Ruth met a Navy man and they were married in the late 1950's. They had six children, Thomas, Daniel, Gail, Mary, John, and Wayne. Their father's name was Romeo Langlois. After many years they were divorced. Ruth remarried to Francis Farrell and they settled in Grafton, Massachusetts, and had one son, Jimmy.

Her aunt Albina and uncle Arthur Boucher adopted Barbara Peterson born in 1929. They lived in Easthampton, Massachusetts. Barbara married Paul Gelinas who served in the United States Navy and they had four children, Suzanne, Ronald, Rodney and another daughter and settled in Easthampton, Massachusetts.

Jane Peterson met John Cronin in the early 1950's and was married soon after. They had four children, John, Judy, Danny and Joyce and they settled in Millbury, Massachusetts, moved to Florida for a brief stay and returned to Shrewsbury, Massachusetts.

During the Great Depression William Peterson, Jr., was in the bootlegging business. He would take 2 of his boys with him in his touring car to deliver the booze, which was wrapped in newspapers. He never took any more than the two boys at a time with him. He was arrested several times and received jail time on three occasions. 1934 was the last time we saw William. He had visited us once at the Hartford County Home. After that visit he moved our mother to Massachusetts. We never saw him again.

The second family that William started was in 1934 when he married Vera Caroline Nowak in Lowell, Massachusetts. He was now known as William Lawrence Donovan. They had three children, John, Patricia and Gail, born in 1937, 1939 and 1942.

John attended many colleges, such as Boston University, The Hartford Institute of Accounting, Territorial College of Guam, Eastern Washington University, and eventually graduated with a Bachelor's degree from Eastern Washington University in 1974. He also received his Master's in Business Administration in 1978 from the same school.

In the time from his first college attendance he served in the United States Air Force for over 30 years, 12 in active duty and 18 in the United States Reserves and Air National Guard retiring in 1985 as a Master Sergeant. He served in Guam, Marianna Islands, Lackland Air Force Base, Larson Air Force Base, Fairchild Air Force Base and England Air Force Base. He married Judith Mayfield in Coeur D'Alene, Idaho and had three children, Michele, John and Mark. He is now retired an residing in Deer Park, Washington.

Patricia Carol Donovan was married to Ken Mann who was the only chief senior airline pilot for American Airlines and passed early into the marriage. They had one child, Daniel. Patricia is now retired and lives in Seymour, Connecticut.

Gail Lorraine Donovan was married three times and had three children, Anthony, Carol Ann and Marne. Her last husband, Peter DelFranco died. One ironic thing about Peter is that he was born on the same day as I was, November 7, 1937. She resides in Stratford, Connecticut with her son and is retired.

Now let us see what happened to the four wives of William Peterson, AKA Donovan. Isabelle Seymour, William's first wife as you know was left to fend for her and the remaining four children in 1933. To take care of her and the children she had to go to work and worked first of all at a felt mill in Millbury, Massachusetts, which manufactured felt goods for the United States Army and Navy. She later worked for the Wauskanut Woolen mill in Farnumsville, Massachusetts. She also received monthly allotment checks from all her sons in the military between 1941 and 1945. Isabelle lived in South Grafton, Massachusetts for 55 years and passed away on October 15, 1989 at the age of 88.

William's second wife, Vera Caroline Nowak didn't fair much better than his first wife Isabelle. Vera was left behind by William (now his surname is Donovan) about 1946 or 1947. The home that they owned at 365 Ruth Street, Bridgeport, Connecticut off course was lost, and Vera and her two daughters had to fend for themselves. They went on State welfare and lived in State subsidized houses or apartments for many years. Vera had to go to work to make ends meet and went to work for Sikorsky Aircraft, first in Bridgeport, Connecticut and later in their new plant in Stratford, Connecticut. By this time they were living at 512 Harral Avenue, Bridgeport, Connecticut in subsidized apartments or better known as the "projects". Son John had joined the family in mid 1951 and attended high school in Bridgeport, Connecticut and college later at Boston University and the Hartford Institute of Accounting. He joined the United States Air Force in June of 1956. Vera continued to work for Sikorsky's until early retirement at age 59 or about 1969. She then retired to Florida and stayed there for a long period of time, returning to Stratford, Connecticut to be close to her daughters. She just recently celebrated her 97th birthday and is in the Lord Chamberlain Rest Home and Re-hab center.

Not much is known about Agnes Hael Southworth after her marriage to William in 1956. He left her within a month of the marriage for her to fend for herself. He must have seen her again as Patricia Donovan, William's daughter by Vera stated she saw them after 1956 at Agnes's home in East Granby, Connecticut. The only other piece of information lies in her death certificate in which is stated that she was a widow, which indicates that she knew that William passed away in 1982.

The fourth wife, Marjorie Hecht we have covered in detail in a previous chapter. It appeared that William and Marjorie had a good life and enjoyed each other for many years starting back in 1955 when William first met Marjorie until William's death in 1982.

Chapter 6   THE SUMMARY

In summary, William was first a farmer, and then he became a soldier and engineer, a bootlegger, a womanizer, a lover and inventor and other things not to be mentioned in this book.

He led a long, hurtful, and industrious life, with four wives, and 14 children. All of the children had good and long lives; some of the first children are still living although time had taken many of them away. The second set of children are all retired and living a good life. It can be said that the wives all took the "bull by the horn" and succeed in life. The same can be said for all the children who made it through all the hardships they all endured, in some cases for many, many years. This book tried to give a true and accurate representation of all the many individuals involved in William's life history, and to show how life goes on even through many hardships. I might note that William's nickname was "Wild Bill", which is noted in the title of this book, and surely this story is amazing, and his nickname fits.

Some of William's children were not treated well, and some of the children did dislike him, but others did forgive him for all the misery he caused his wives and the children. There was a reunion in 2002 with the children of both marriages and that went very well. All the ones who came to the reunion were nice folks and all had a good time. Some of the children have kept in touch with the others.

In retrospect all came out pretty good with the children and the wives that were involved with William Peterson, AKA William Donovan. Time has healed all wounds and in most cases William has been forgiven.

Finally, I want to thank all persons who participated in writing of this book and dedicate the book to first of all to all four wives of William who persevered his antics. Secondly I wish to thank Henry (Hank) and Eileen Peterson for filling in the gaps in the book that I had no knowledge. Thirdly I want to thank Richard Lambert for all the genealogical research that he worked on, and believe me it was extensive. Fourth, I would like to thank Elizabeth Lewin for providing me with information on the last twelve years of William's life in Arizona.

I want to end this book with an appropriate poem:
"Elusive Kinsman"

Alas, my elusive kinsman
You've led me quite a chase
I thought I'd found your courthouse
But the Yankees burned the place
You always kept your bags packed
Although you had no fame, and
Just for the fun of it
Twice you changed your name
You never owed any man, or
At least I found no bills
In spite of eleven offspring
You never left a will
They say our names's from Europe
Came state side on a ship
Either they lost the passenger list
Or granddad gave them the slip

I'm the only one looking
Another searcher I can't find
I pray (maybe that's his fathers name)
As I go out of my mind
They said you had a headstone
In a shady plot
I've been there twenty times, and
Can't even find the lot
You never wrote a letter
Your Bible we can't find
It's probably in some attic
Out of sight and out of mind
You first married a ….Smith
And just to set the tone
The other four were Sarahs
And everyone a Jones
You cost me two fortunes
One of which I did not have
My wife, my house and Fido
How I miss that yellow lab
But somewhere you slipped up,
Ole Boy, Somewhere you left a track
And if I don't find you this year
Well…..Next year I'll be back!
Original poem by Wayne Hand – Printed by permission

*

www.ingramcontent.com/pod-product-compliance
Lightning Source LLC
Chambersburg PA
CBHW031433040426
42444CB00006B/789